SHE

❖

PATRICE SIMPSON

Falmouth, Jamaica

Copyright © 2020
Author & Publisher: Patrice A. Simpson
ISBN: 978-976-8277-86-2
National Library Of Jamaica

First Printing: Kingston, Jamaica (2020)

TABLE OF CONTENTS

AUTHOR'S NOTE

SHE is a collection of vignettes inspired by the lives and struggles of real women. Each piece was written from the heart with lots of love and understanding. The idea was created to touch the topics realistically so the emotions are truly felt.

Women struggle everyday with low self-esteem, physical abuse, and a lack of self-love. Sometimes we forget that we have a voice we can use to inspire other women around us, women who share the same struggles and cannot seem to find their way out.

I have used my God-given talent to create these vignettes to reach out to my fellow women, to let them know that it is okay to struggle. We all go through something in life but we can all be victors if only we believe in our capabilities. I encourage all my readers to think positively through all adversities, no matter how hard they may seem to be.

ACKNOWLEDGMENTS

I would like to express sincere gratitude to my Creator for blessing me with the talent of writing. I am happy to be able to express myself with words on paper.

A special thank you to my family and dear friends for being great confidants and mentors. I appreciate all the kind words, constructive criticism, and encouragement that you shared with me. Heartfelt thanks to my darling son, Rozayn, for being my biggest motivation.

Lastly, thank you to the women around me who have inspired me to write these stories.

A SOLID WOMAN

She is strong; she is beautiful.
She is amazing; she is wonderful. She is very
humble; she is very sweet. She sweeps me
off my feet.

She is a princess, an empress.
A queen that is uplifting and honest. She
faces a lot, sweat, tears, and pain.
She's never defeated, nor does she
complain.

She is joyful; she is fun to be around.
She is playful, but she firmly stands her
ground. She is music; she is the dance.
She is strength, humility, endurance.

QUESTIONS OF THE HEART

She watches you while you sleep and dries the sweat from your forehead, she tolerates your snoring even though it is really loud. She watches you inhale and exhale while you toss and turn; she comforts you because you may be having a bad dream. You steal all the covers and she wishes she could steal them all back and let you freeze to death. She doesn't because she loves you. She tolerates everything because she cares. It's 1 a.m. and the silence is deafening; she cannot sleep.

She is up thinking, praying, hoping that her dreams won't be crushed in the blink of an eye. She faces the silence; she hears the slow yet sure beating of your heart. She wonders, she ponders. Does he love her? Does he love her as much as she loves him? Does he love her more? Is this just another one of his games? Silly, stupid, childish games. Does he understand the concept of a heart not wanting to be broken? Does he even care?

Silence. Pure deadly silence as she feels her heart slowly, slowly, slowly shatter. She focuses her attention back to him, the man she loves, the man she cares so deeply for, the man who betrayed her. She contemplates the pain of the past, a journey of lust, lies, and deceit. She thinks, "Why is it so easy for men to get away with everything ? Why do I easily give in? Why do I forgive? Why do I break down my walls to the blatant occurrences? Why am I so weak? Why can't I be strong?"

Silence as the tears stream down her cheeks. She thinks, she ponders, she wonders, she cries, she laughs. She laughs hysterically, cries even louder, laughs again. She slowly wipes her tears and drifts off into a deep sleep, a place of solitude, a place of peace.

A WOMAN SCORNED

She hurts. She hides it though; she does not want him to see her cry, to see her weak. Silence. Darkness. Fear. In the midst of it all, she tries to gain some comfort, some security, by loving herself first. How could he have loved her? How could he have cared for her?

Why did she fall so easily for his empty promises? Why did she turn a blind eye to his inconsistency? Was it because she loved him? Yes, but it was never only that. She had invested years, sweat, tears, her heart, her body, her mind, her soul, her dreams.

Everything she was, she gave him and still, it was never enough. She dug deep, isolated herself, meditated. She hungered for closure. But why was she torturing herself in thinking he'd come around, in thinking he'd apologize, in thinking he'd change, for good, for himself, for her, for them, for an amazing life together. She contemplated. Her mind got tired. She contemplated some more. She came up with a solution.

She would close the door herself on that chapter of her life; she would not wait for him anymore. Why would she? A man who is incapable of seeing what is right in front of him will always be blind unless drastically shaken by reality. She had two choices, hold on and never grow or let the hell go and glow. By letting go, she also knew she was doing him a huge favor, she was allowing him to go search for something he would never find again. She knew ; he didn't. And that's how it would be.

She was a good woman, her loyalty ran deep; she was unchangeable, she was courageous, she was determined to love herself unconditionally. She knew she never really lost, but he did. She won because she learned, she conquered, she triumphed. She was a woman of dignity. She would witness this man, who had never appreciated her, cry his heart out a few years down the road, trying to mend things that were obviously meant to stay broken. He would be too late. She knew. He didn't. And that's how it would be. She smiled at the thought and said one word, "Karma."

A GOOD WOMAN IS HARD TO FIND

She tries to speak, to let it all out; she wants to forget the pain. She is dumbfounded, lost, hurting. She is a woman filled with resentment, regrets, and fear. She no longer laughs in her reality. It's a moment of silence for her. Her emotions are unstable, her head is not in the right place, filled with random, sad thoughts. She's left with the question, "Is it me?"

He doesn't show that he loves her; he doesn't show an ounce of regret. He doesn't seem to care that he has caused her unforgettable pain, sleepless nights, tears. Through it all, she still tries to see a dim light, a speck of hope; hope that one day she'll forgive him completely, hope that one day she'll live with no regrets or fear of the future, hope that one day she'll rely on her judgment, will love herself enough to know her worth. He broke her. He broke everything she was. He turned her smiles into frowns, her happiness into sorrows, her heart ice cold.

She digs deep, isolates herself from the harsh reality that he broke her. He diminished her self-esteem, made her lose sight of who she really was. A good woman, who was indeed hard to find. She would always be a good woman. She was a rare diamond amid regular pebbles; she was a keeper. Would he be man enough to wise up and keep her?

LETTING GO

He needs space, he tells her. They need to take a break; things aren't as they planned them to be. But really is that all? He leaves her wondering. He leaves her heartbroken. He leaves her confused. What he hopes to gain from it all, she does not know.

Love. The one word in her life that she questions the most. Did she ever give love? Did she ever receive real love? Does she even know what love is? Betrayal, pain, abuse, deceit, loneliness: these words she knows. These words built her, made her hard, her heart stone-cold. No wonder he cannot love her, no wonder he cannot give her his all, he sees that she is weak. She has not yet mastered self-love, she needs to find herself, she needs to first find who she is.

She writes. It helps to release the tension she feels, it helps to calm her mind. She reaches for a pen and a piece of paper. She writes one word. She begins to sob quietly, until she can no longer hold it in. The weight on her shoulders is too much of a burden, so she cries, a little louder than she normally would.

She has just written one word, yet the tears write the entire story.

Years filled with regrets, loss: love lost, friends lost, dreams lost, hope lost. How can she regain it all? How can she even begin to pick up the pieces? She does not know. She just feels like giving up, she just feels unworthy. Every day she lives a lie, she pretends to be happy, she pretends to be healed of the scars, like nothing bothers her.

She is done pretending. It is time. Time to not pretend, but time to truly heal. It hurt her, but she also has to thank him. Thank him for know- ing her more than she knew herself. She decides it is finally the time to just let things flow.

ADDICTED TO MR. WRONG

He gives her attention, an ounce of satisfaction she has been long- ing to receive; he understands her; he knows just what to do and say to make her feel better. He's kind, smart, loving, supportive, and makes her his priority. But her heart is not with him. She feels stuck, torn, unsure, and confused.

She compares him to the one who has her heart. He is everything Mr. Wrong isn't, everything she's yearned for, everything she's needed, everything she's deserved. Why can't she love him back? Why can she not even try? Why does she withdraw from being loved the right way? Her heart, her heart won't let her. Her mind, her mind won't let her. Her body, her body won't let her.

Mr. Wrong has cemented himself in her heart and her mind. He's left her with memories she just cannot forget. He touched her body like no other man had before; she submitted to him and he had taken charge. It was more than sex, more than love, she just couldn't explain it. She was high on him and no other. Nobody understood why, neither did she herself. He still owns her; she cannot escape. All she knows, is that she cannot let go. At least, not yet.

Time would have to be on her side. To guide her, to heal her, to strengthen her, to make her once more an emotionally independent woman. Time would have to help her become the woman she was destined to be.

FINDING WHO WE ARE

She is tired. Not physically, but spiritually, emotionally drained. Weak. Vulnerable. Not at peace. She keeps asking the universe, "Why me?" She could not see the light at the end of the tunnel, the rainbow beneath the stormy skies. Happiness. She wondered what that word meant to her anymore. She was doing well, better than most you could say, excelling in areas she once saw herself unfit to start the journey. Something was missing though.

She did not know what was missing or even how to obtain it. She didn't even have the drive to find out what it was. "What's the sense in being motivated to end up being disappointed," she thought to herself. Her friends and family encouraged her to try, but what was a woman to do whose life was filled with nothing but disappointments?

It's like we eventually become victims of our circumstances unknowingly. It's like she, you, me, a woman, a mother, a sister, a friend, the brokenhearted, the neglected, the unappreciated, the abused, the scarred, the diamonds in their own rough, in their most devastated form. We can't give you definite advice on being an all-woman, a whole person, because we are yet to find who we truly are.

DEPRESSION IS REAL

When she was happy, she wrote. When she was sad, she wrote. Writing healed her, it made her whole. She was going through a phase she had promised herself to never let happen again. A few years ago she was struck down by depression, almost lost it all, her life included. That had been the worst of her, it was her ultimate downfall. Pain, betrayal, deceit. She never understood the cause of her pain, the root of all her problems, it was inexplicable. The overthinking, the crying out in great agony, the constant torture of her fears got the best of her. She had been weak; she had been stupid; she had attempted to take her own life. Nobody understood. She was at that very same spot now. Who could she talk to? Who could she trust? Who would understand? She did not even understand herself. What it was, she did not know, but something inside her made her unhappy, something was missing and she could not put a finger on it.

People were beginning to notice her weight loss, they were beginning to see the sadness beneath her smile; she also felt it. She was lost, she needed purpose, she needed to see the light, even the slightest ray of hope. She needed peace. All she ever wanted was to be happy. She had done her best, she had tried to be a good person, so why was goodness not being returned to her? Why did she feel like she always had to be fighting? Why was everything so confusing? Why? Why? Why? If someone did know, could they please explain it to her?

AVE MARIA

She needed purpose; she needed security, guidance, compassion, love. She craved peace. It was hard going through each day without a reason, without living out her purpose. She gazed out her window; it was a gloomy morning, the rain was falling. "The sun did not come out to play today,"she thought. She watched the raindrops falling, in a similar pattern to how her tears had fallen. Slowly. More rapidly. Slowly. More rapidly. She had often wondered if the skies were crying when it rained, if the clouds just got so sad, they couldn't hold the emotions anymore. She watched the raindrops, she listened to them; she reached out and felt the coolness of the rain on her tired hands.

If only the rain could just wash away all her pain, worries, and sorrows. If only the rain could consume her and make her whole, if only. She had been through it; she had witnessed it all. All she wanted was to be truly happy again, but instead she beat herself up, she held on to too much, she sometimes forgot she was only human.

She breathed an air of freshness, in and out. She inhaled and exhaled. She sat by the window watching the raindrops, contemplating. Her deep thinking was interrupted by the vibration of her phone. It was her daily reminder of "positive quotes." She opened the app and the quote read, "The rain may pour, but soon the sun will shine again." She smiled. How did an app know exactly what to say? But it was right, she'd just have to ride out the rainy days. Pitter patter. Pitter patter. Pitter patter, the raindrops hit the ground. She closed her window, went by her sofa, and knelt. She was going to pray. A powerful prayer, a prayer filled with faith.

BEAUTIFUL LIAR

She had despised the other women. She would have made them suffer if she had gotten the chance. Her thoughts had been so dark and destructive. She had been filled with unfiltered rage and regrets. She'd wanted to scream, shatter glass, and then use the pieces to cut her wrists. She'd wanted to see the blood flow as though it was coming from her bro- ken heart. She had been depressed, suicidal, at wit's end. Until she put her- self in those other women's shoes.

She took the place of these women who were craving affection and felt what they felt, heard what they heard, and believed what they believed. It was then that she realized how hard and complicated life could be for a woman. How easy it was for a man to sweep a lonely woman off her feet, how easy it was for a woman to fall for a chain of lies and deceit. She knew there was no sense in hating the other women to whom he had given a piece of himself, because, just like her, they never got him as a whole.
They got a facade, a mix of different personalities that would have been perfect if they were true. They got a liar, a cheater, a manipulator, a cowardly fraud. A wolf in sheep's clothing, a mere pretender who cared for nobody else but himself.

FLY, BUTTERFLY, FLY!

She'd been through hell and back. She struggled. She fought the good fight. With hidden tears of the heart, she still found the courage to utter, "I'm okay." Life chewed her up and spat her out, yet still she stood undefeated. She knew there was more to life, she knew she had a greater purpose; she was a caterpillar evolving into a butterfly. Aging gracefully, her beauty glowed.

She had a beautiful heart. She tried to positively touch the lives of the people she met. She gave without expecting anything in return, loved unconditionally, and forgave wholeheartedly. She was just trying to mend the broken pieces in her life, correct her mistakes, and make the very best of every day.

She was a woman determined to rise, find her path, and work on becoming the best version of herself. She knew obstacles would come, stumbling blocks would try to trip her, negative spirits would try to hold her back. But after all she'd been through, she undoubtedly knew she'd overcome.

BEAUTIFULLY CRAFTED

She was a broken vase, shattered to the core and stripped of her outer beauty, but she was perfect. She was the epitome of a true survivor. No matter what life threw at her, she overcame and that was her true beauty. She was always humble in her life experiences, and grateful for even the smallest blessings. Time had been her teacher, and the struggles she lived through had been her tests, but regardless, she triumphed over them.

She laid in bed reminiscing on all the friends who had left her behind, all those who had left her stranded. All those who had walked out of her life when she needed them the most. She shook her head and smiled. They were not meant to know the new her, the person she had turned out to be, the newfound woman. She wasn't holding a grudge though, she really wished the very best for them.

She was loving the journey and all it had to offer. The good, the bad, the happy, the sad, the beautiful, the ugly. Ying and yang. It was perfection, the ideal balance of life. Her heart was clean, her intentions were true, and her vibe was pure. She was a diamond in the rough, gorgeously crafted and one in a million.

RUNNING OUT OF PATIENCE

It was not that she didn't love him, but there was no spark anymore; she had outgrown him and all that he was, all he thrived to be. Sometimes she felt guilty because he had stood by her in some rough moments, truth be told. He had been an amazing friend. Sometimes he had been more than a friend, more than a lover. Sometimes, she felt liberated because there was a point in time when she had loved him even more than she loved herself.

It was bittersweet, a part of her had hoped he would turn out to be the man of her dreams. A part of her had also yearned for independence. She felt as though she was ready for something he was incapable of. She had reached that part of the journey where he no longer had a purpose in her life. Her mind was all over the place. Happy thoughts, sad thoughts. Past thoughts, future thoughts.

There was something inside of her that needed ignition, no one understood but her how important her ambitions were. She no longer needed a man, but a partner, a lifelong commitment between two people working on their goals and triumphing over obstacles. Sometimes her mind wandered into the distance and she had to snap back to reality; she had so many unanswered questions. The only advice she could give herself was "Wait and see how it all turns out," but another part of her believed she had waited long enough.

THE FIGHTER

She often had to question life, asking why. Why her? Why not the woman seated beside her? When bad things happened, they had been repetitive, one after other. Downfall after downfall, heartbreak after heartbreak, disappointment after disappointment. It took her years to realize why it all had to happen to her. It was one moment. One moment breathing , being alive and well.

She woke up, hair uncombed, no makeup on, no clothes on, and stood bare in front of the mirror. She confronted herself, as pure as she was, with thoughts as raw and unfiltered as she could stand. She felt herself shaking, the emotions within her were too powerful for her to even utter a word. She used both hands to hug her waist, resisting the urge to wipe away her tears.

She stood crying, looking at her image in the smeared mirror. She needed to see herself cry and she did. That was how she gained her strength. That was how she understood why bad things had happened to her. Beneath the tears, beyond the image in the mirror, stood a fighter. A fighter not obvious to anyone else but her. A silent fighter within.

INHALE, EXHALE

She felt good. It was good. Even though it was bad, it was good. She was proud of who she was and she would embrace all her flaws. It took mistake after mistake for her to finally see her worth and find her strength. A few years back, she would not have known what life was doing for her. It was through all these trials that she had become a stronger person. She had to thank the past, even though she would not linger there; she had to revisit memory lane at times and thank the experiences for grooming her.

She had a dream. She saw herself standing by the ocean, inhaling fresh air and releasing the negativity within her. She felt the smooth sand beneath her tired feet, appreciating the whole scenery with awe. The water, however, seemed to be angry that she was there because it was rough and dirty.

She stepped into it, washing her feet. The more she washed, the calmer the water became. The more in tune she was with nature, the more in tune nature was with her.

She sat and meditated. She felt as though many more trials were yet to come. Even if everything else seemed perfect, one aspect might not be. Just like the water. But she also knew that, in life, it was all about the choices we make. She decided to react to everything positively. She wrote inhale exhale in the sand, and slowly, slowly awoke from her sleep.

UNREQUITED LOVE

He watched her from a distance, a beautiful woman. She did not even know that it was her scars that made her beautiful. He wanted to say something , anything , but all he could do was admire her beauty from afar. There she was, with the same man who did not appreciate her; he was apologizing for the hundredth time, and she was swept away once more. He wondered, "Why does she let that happen? Does she not know her worth?"

She needed saving, someone to sweep her off her feet and never let her fall. He had the urge to break up the temporary reunion and false portrayal of love, but he held back. That was not the right way. He had sent her a note along with beautiful flowers, red roses to be exact. He had overheard that they were her favorite and they had made her smile. Too bad she didn't know who they were from; maybe her man took all the praise.

He felt stupid; she was not his, but she was more than perfect in his eyes. He did many things to her in his mind. He had to snap back to reality, he was moving way too fast. All he had to do was wait. Wait in the shadows, until he obtained the courage to chase her. He hoped one day she could be with him, for her heart was not his, and that was the sad part, for his heart was hers.

DREAMS DO MATTER

She wrote. There was a fire burning within her to express herself so she put her words on paper. It was as if she had to, she did not even understand why, but she had to.

However, she had to be in the zone, she had to literally feel the raw emotions.

The writing was one with her. She gave life to every piece. She gave each piece a voice, a part of her. Writing had become her therapy, her love and her soul. She had always dreamt of touching many lives, leaving something with everyone for them to remember. She was drawn to those who were broken because they had the best stories to tell and they were the best to relate to the voice she put on paper.

She laid in bed, unsure of where the journey was taking her but trusting it nevertheless. She thought, "If the universe wants me to write, I'm going to write and I'm going to be damn good at it!" She sighed, relaxing her mind while enjoying the eloquence of her words. It was way past her bedtime but that was fine, for her current reality was already like living a dream.

SEXUALLY CONFUSED

She sometimes fought feelings she could not comprehend. She was faced with many adversities but this was one of her hardest. The abused are normally scarred in a way that only people with true compassion can understand.

She was a little girl who had encountered many occasions deemed fit only for adults. She was a little girl who was sometimes confused about her sexuality. Women had touched her, pleasured her, and it was good. Sometimes her mind wandered to an empty space, questioning the possibility of making love to the next beautiful woman who came in contact with her.

But that wasn't who she was, was it? Were her experiences clouding her judgment? Did she not know right from wrong ? Why did she get so caught up in the moment only to later have regrets? Or was she over thinking? She needed freedom from the past, that was for sure and she was the only one who could give that to herself.

ONE STEP AT TIME

She was getting there, but she couldn't tell exactly where. All she knew was she had to pour her heart out and give it her best shot. Give it all she had. There was a fire roaring inside her, an inexplicable hunger, an unquenchable thirst for something big.

She was changing from the inside out; it was as though her darkened soul had seen the light. There was joy, there were tears. There was peace. Through all the pain, she had persevered and conquered her demons. She was standing alone yet she felt as though there were a thousand soldiers behind her.

Her heart was full. This time not of stones, but of love. Self-love was the most important element. She sat on her wicker chair staring through her bedroom window; she watched as the leaves on the trees slowly swayed in the wind and she felt at ease. She spoke to the wind, "Where is my destiny taking me?"

A little robin beneath the leaves chirped away, as if responding to her question. She knew regardless of her fears, the journey had to be completed. She had to become whole and to do so, she needed to take things one step at a time.

WAITING IN VAIN

She stayed up waiting. It seemed to be the only thing she could do. Wait. Wait on him to love her right, wait on him to take her emotions seriously. Wait. Yes she loved him, so she could wait, but she was running out of patience.

Every time he made a mistake, there was a burning sensation inside of her that she knew was the hurt surfacing again. She knew it was her heart breaking once more. She was so tired of it, words could not even explain. He had asked her to be patient, to give him some time to make things right, but she believed that he was only taking her for granted.

She could be wrong, he could indeed be the love of her life; after all, nobody was perfect. But on the other hand, she could be right and needed to dodge a stupid bullet. And that was life, unpredictable. She vowed that she would always expect the unexpected, but still live as though nothing bothered her.

LIVE IN THE MOMENT

She had sex with him even though she was upset by his actions. Wasn't that going to make things more complicated? Wasn't the woman the one who got more attached after sexual intercourse? She knew all this, but regardless, her body could not say no. She gave in, she allowed him to pleasure her.

He made sweet love to her while looking deeply in her eyes, never once taking his attention from her. They held on to each other like they were the only two people in the world, reaching their points, embracing passionately. Then they were done. He held her for a while and placed a soft kiss on her forehead.

Everything was perfect for a moment. Just a moment. She was truly pleased until she was harshly struck back into reality. "That's the thing about living in the moment, just enjoy every minute while it lasts, because it doesn't last forever," she thought sadly.

CAN'T RAISE A MAN

She was told she had work to do. She needed to change him and help him become more than who he was. She needed to be the woman who pushed him to become successful. She was pressured into believing that was her sole purpose in the relationship: to make him better, to complete him in their eyes. But they forgot, she needed to work on herself, too. She needed time to find herself, too.

She was judged endlessly by imperfect beings, frowned upon when she could not exceed their expectations. But in truth, what woman have you known to change a man? Doesn't a man grow up on his own? Is it not the man's decision to yearn and achieve success? And even sometimes with a good woman beside him, a man still falters. She knew this. She had seen it happen many times before.

She failed, but it was okay, because above it all, she was happy. Whether or not they accepted her. She cared zero if she didn't make the cut. She was growing and glowing , and all she could do was pray for him. Pray that he'd find his true purpose because she had been lost once too, so she certainly understood. She would take no blame for a man's actions, none whatsoever. The only actions she was responsible for were her own.

A HIDDEN VOICE

She never knew how good a story was until she shared it. She never knew she could be an inspiration to others. She never knew she had a voice. A voice that was hidden, but held so much purpose, so much power, so much promise. She never knew writing could give such healing, healing from things she had never found any other antidote for.

Writing became a medium through which she could share her most intimate thoughts, her go to in times of confusion. It was through her writing that she understood why she went through bad things in her life. She needed a story, and not just any story, she needed a triumphant one. So she would write, even in her most devastated form, because the thing about writing words on paper is you can make them into something beautiful.

FALLEN SOLDIER

She remembered the day of his funeral vividly. It felt like only yesterday, even though many years had gone by. He had been one of her favorites, even though everyone had grown up and moved apart. He would always be remembered as one of her most important cousins.

Losing a family member so loved was one of the hardest things she had to encounter in her life. Some would call it a cliché, but she truly believed that he was her guardian angel. He had helped her surpass many obstacles, in other words, he did not die in vain. That was what she told herself to cope.

She would never forget him. She would keep the memories of him in her heart for forever and a day. She would always speak of him, so his name would resonate in the ears of many. And she would continuously hope and pray that he, indeed, was resting in peace.

SOMETHING TO REMEMBER

Her writing was authentic, unique and different. Her words touched souls, ignited feelings of joy, offered rays of hope. Her words flowed as gently as a silent stream, soothing the mind and lifting one's spirit. She was not your typical writer who wrote for fun, money or fame. Writing was her passion, her therapy. Every piece she shared was a part of her. She was a giver, not expecting anything in return.

Life is a journey we are allowed to take only once, she thought it was important to leave something behind. Some words of hope that could truly help someone in a dark time. Something they could remember, hold on to, and keep tucked in their hearts forever. Stories shared and treasured, because they were not just words on paper, but real-life events of true survivors.

A "WE" MENTALITY

She was not supposed to talk, she was often silenced. Her tongue had bled from words left unsaid, things she had to chew up and push right back down her throat. As a result of this she kept a lot of thoughts to herself, so there were many issues bottled up inside her. And to top it all off, he did not care. As long as he got the last word, as long as he won the battle, as long as he was right, everything was good.

Most of their arguments started because of miscommunication. One person only listening to reply or not listening at all, thus missing the point. But relationships were all about listening, weren't they? Compromise? Teamwork? A "we" mentality not an "I"? She had often checked herself and apologized over and over again for her flaws when she did mess up. But most times, she felt as though she was walking on eggshells, hoping she wouldn't say the wrong thing or offend him.

She tried not to crush his ego and create unnecessary drama. But what good is a woman if she can't even motivate the man she loves? And what good is a man who refuses to even try and listen?

HOLD ON, LET GO

She was here yet again. She felt deeply hurt. She should have known, nothing would change. Was she blind? Had she not seen it countless times before? Trusting a man, believing his words, taking one step forward to take two steps back. Empty promises. Shattered dreams. Disappointment, resentment.

Some people told her to wait a while because things take time to heal. But deep in her heart there was something tugging at her, telling her she had waited long enough. Nobody understood and nobody could ever feel what she felt. She was constantly fighting a losing battle, holding on to a mere illusion. She needed to trust and let go. Let things truly flow. Leave the relationship and solely focus on herself, no matter what he said or how he begged her to stay. She needed peace. She craved security. She had to accept the fact that sometimes you just had to let go.

WHAT IF

She screamed. He hit her harder. This time in her flawless face with an object so sharp it left a scar. For the hundredth time, he hit her. Many times before the scars weren't physical, for everyone to see. It had been her heart that he bruised, broke, and tainted.

Her mental health had suffered severely. On days when she felt like she could not keep going , she had to find solace in the eyes of her children. Some would tell her, "Leave him! Let him be!" But they didn't know the sweet, tender man who would come back with roses, kisses, and a physical connection so strong she would forget the pain, would lose herself in him all over again.

He wasn't always a monster, that's what she would tell herself continuously. But, what if, in a split second he went too far? What if he held her by the throat just for a minute too long ? What then? And really, what's love got to do with it?

SECRET LOVERS

She knew he couldn't make it official. No one could know they dated, not even the slightest hint could be given away. They'd spend some time together, have sex, then he would go home to his wife. The sex was great although it only lasted for a short while. Everything had to be done on time, his timing not hers. She sometimes felt frustrated, deep in her heart. She wanted more. More of him, more of their physical exchange, more of his heart, but she couldn't have him because they had made an arrangement. She was nothing more than a secret, a sad, lonely secret.

His heart was at home no matter what he said, no matter how much she gave him. And if she got him for herself, she'd lose him the same way his wife did...to another woman. Because life is a cycle isn't it? We get what we give and there ain't no other way around it.

PHILOPHOBIA

She started building walls again, hard, well cemented. He started building walls, too. What stood between them was something both could conquer, by just saying , "I love you". But ego was a hell of a thing. Or maybe, "I'm sorry?" Something , anything.

She sat within the barrier lonely and confused, waiting for him to make a move. They say men are naturally hunters and they normally go after what they want. So she waited on him to make the first move; it was the right way. He did, but she was still not pleased.

Why was she not satisfied? Why could she not see the good intentions he had toward her? What was it? Paranoia? Insecurity? Amid the mistakes, he really did love her. What her problem was, she truly didn't know. Was she suffering from the been-there-done-that-shit syndrome? She just had to figure it out, before it was too late.

FOOL FOR LOVE

He told her to leave him alone but she couldn't. She was a woman who had not yet mastered self-reliance, self-respect, or self-love. No matter what insults he threw at her, she'd still pursue him, because in her fantasy, he was her knight in shining armor. The Prince Charming to her Cinderella. He loved her, he just didn't know it yet.

To her it was something to smile about, but for others, looking in from the outside, it was sad and unfortunate. And that's the thing , people have different perspectives when it comes to the word love. Her love was defined by abuse, constant disrespect, and mockery, but then he'd be nice again, so that was what made it okay.
But in all truth, who are they to tell her that she's wrong, when they haven't seen life through her eyes, or felt what she has felt?

NOT YET OVER

She knew that the heroine sometimes needed some saving , too. No matter how many situations she handled well, there were some she'd never fix on her own because they were not meant to be repaired. Life had its ways, creating barriers, building walls, placing stumbling blocks in her path. She sometimes could not comprehend the journey or what it was that life wanted from her.

She accepted pain as though it was one with her, learning to embrace it, learning to fight everything that tried to hold her back. Her soul was darkened, a moment of sadness, silence, doubt, and confusion. But in the midst of the turmoil, she still felt her heart beating, reminding her that it was not yet over. She just had to keep pushing.

STRONG WOMAN

She listened to her grandmother, a woman of experience, endless knowledge, and wisdom. She lingered on every word, finding the true meaning behind the stories her grandmother told her, savoring every lesson she was meant to learn.

There was one word that was consistent through it all: strength. She knew no matter what life threw at her, she had to keep her faith and find her own strength. She watched her grandmother as she laid on her sickbed. Ailments had tried to overpower her but she was not broken. Every word she spoke held immense pride and power. Regardless of the difficulties she faced in her life, she was indeed a strong woman. It was in that moment she knew exactly who she wanted to be and it was nothing short of a strong, unapologetic woman.

CREATE NEW MEMORIES

She had to learn to forgive herself. She had to accept the fact that she was not perfect, that her flaws made her unique. She had a really good heart, even though sometimes she did some really bad things. But coming to terms with her mistakes was one thing, facing them was another.

She had a conscience, and this was the reason she beat herself up. Having a conscience and knowing the right thing sometimes made her forget that she was only human. Some things she wished she had done better, some days she wished she had lived more productively, but what could she change?

All those moments were long gone and she truly needed to let go and start creating new chapters, new stories. And that's exactly what she did. She poured out her raw emotions, the present, and hopes for the future with a broken pencil on a torn piece of paper.

POSITIVE THINKING ONLY

She deserved happiness and she would give herself nothing short of that. She deserved to smile and laugh for no reason, because of all the bad things she'd gone through. She deserved peace above all, the peace to move forward and leave the past behind.

There was one important detail that she acquired while on her journey and it made her powerful: she learned how to control her mind, her everyday thoughts, and play on them. Throwing the irrelevant out, dimming the way for negativity, doubt, fear, or confusion.

She chose to solely focus on the good in every situation no matter how hard it was. She had the power. She held the key to her own happiness. She was the only person responsible for her peace of mind, her well being. So it was mind over matter, and if she didn't mind, then it didn't matter.

GREAT THINGS TAKE TIME

She felt at ease. She was proud. She was satisfied. She was winning. She was getting better. She was trusting the journey and savoring the moments. She had been in a very dark place, unable to move, chained by the regrets of the past. She had lost sight of the power she possessed deep within her.

But time, being the master of all things should never be under-estimated. Time heals, time recompenses. Great things need time and the right time would always be on time. As she regained her power, she became unstoppable. She began to learn new things about herself, exploring all the possibilities of who she could be. She knew she was created for a special purpose, not the ordinary, not the typical, but something supernatural.

SOLITUDE

When she could not explain how she felt, she wrote it down instead. The pencil would sometimes break because of the anger, or the paper would end up crushed and tossed on the floor, but she would start over. She would write again. And she did.

She wrote until her fingers blistered, until the pages would become wet by a story only her swollen eyes could read. The pages understood, they gave her a medium through which she could vent without being judged or shamed. She could scream, whisper, laugh, and cry all at the same time.

Writing was an escape route from reality, a place of solitude in her mind where she was the only one who could enter, a place where her thoughts ran wild, her fears lingered and her peace reigned.

BE PERSISTENT IN PRAYER

She went from zero to one hundred real quick. One minute everything was okay, the next everything was a blur. Doubts over shadowed her dreams. Her self-esteem felt bruised once more. She just never felt as though she was good enough. Enough, the one word she had often tried to be in every aspect of her life. Being a mother, daughter, sister, aunt, friend, and lover. She tried to make everybody happy; she was a giver. She gave so much, she sometimes forgot that she needed to take a break. She needed to relax and rejuvenate, to meet her own needs and do something that she loved.

Sometimes the disappointments were too much. "What does it really take for a girl to just be happy?" she thought. She heard a voice deep inside her utter, "Prayer." Yes, she needed that. Words from the heart that only her Creator could truly comprehend.

A DOMINANT WOMAN

He told her that the other women did not matter; it was her. Always had been, always would be. She was his all and everything. His backbone, his greatest motivation. Just like any other couple, they had their ups and downs, their heated arguments, words they said that they regretted. It was so hard sometimes to see through the pain, but somehow they survived. He would fall back, cease all communication with her until she made the first move.

He was intrigued by their make up sex, so the problems they had never bothered him one bit. She was wild, dominant, and extremely sexy, and he loved it, he craved it. It was in these moments that he felt how much she truly needed and yearned for him. It was much more about getting high off the thought of someone loving every inch and every flaw he had to offer than it ever was about the sex, so he submitted. And with every kiss, with every passionate stroke, he fell for her even more. He was hooked, she had him but he didn't care how sprung he was, because he knew without a doubt that she felt the same.

NOTHING BEATS BEING A MOTHER

Her ultimate goal was to live a happy, comfortable life surrounded by those she loved the most, especially her dear son. Her son was her tower of strength, he was everything a mother wanted her son to be. He exceeded every single expectation that she had of him. He was helpful, polite, and charming.

She sat on her verandah, listening to the sound of the birds in the stillness of the evening. She reminisced on the days when her son was growing inside her. One energetic little boy, filled with lots of kicks and a huge appetite. She smiled at the flashback. Motherhood was indeed an amazing journey. Her favorite memory was when she would sing to him and he would kick hysterically. She would never know if he had loved her singing or hated it but regardless he reacted to the sound of his mother's voice.

She was watching a little boy turn into a man and she would enjoy every moment of the journey. The blessed journey of motherhood. She would be a great mother, supporter, and most importantly a true confidante in hard times.

LOVE IS NO FAIRY TALE

She knew he'd keep hurting her because he didn't know how to love her. He was not ready to go the extra mile, to put her first. She knew this but she still refused to accept it after investing so much into the relationship.

They met when they were only teenagers. They fell in love and it was good for a while. Then everything crashed and burned. Amid the clutter they always found a way to push through, or was that just in her mind? She sometimes felt as though she refused to see the signs. She was holding on to a mere illusion, a fairy tale, a supposed happily ever after story. She knew that sometimes love did conquer all, but she'd also learned that love could cost you everything.

RUNAWAY LOVE

She felt the pain deep within her stomach, she saw the blood. Something was not right. Her instincts told her it was the worst-case scenario but her heart could not accept it. Her baby was leaving her, without being given a name and without a chance to create memories. "Not again!" she screamed, as she held her belly and cried out in great agony.

He was sure to leave her this time; he had threatened that he would. She could not carry a child past the first trimester, she was incapable of giving birth. But he wanted children, he wanted a family. She felt worthless. She curled up on the bed, not giving much thought about soiling the white bedding. He'd be mad, but she didn't care. Just maybe if things were different, maybe if he was much calmer. Maybe if he would stop putting his hands on her, she could bring life into this world. Her thoughts consumed her but one word stood out: leave. She had to. She had to pack her things and run. Cost what it may, the last of her sanity was not worth it.

FINALLY AT PEACE

She fought long. She fought hard. She was not a victor, but she was a fighter. Even when the pain seared through her body and her bones ached, she kept thinking positively. She knew never stopped believing that she could win her battle with this deadly disease.

As her days were prolonged, so was the pain. It slept with her, it ate with her, it consumed her. The pain became one with her until she realized there was no escaping the inevitable. She had to accept her fate and reflect on the person she had been. The journey was a tough one, but it was worth it.

She smiled at the thought of her children, grandchildren, and even her great grandchildren. Her earthly purpose was fulfilled, her job was complete. She was happy, she was finally at peace. She closed her eyes and prepared herself for a deep, deep sleep.

ABUSED GIRL

She was only ten years old when she had her first sexual encounter. He was old enough to be her grandfather. It was as if the days of slavery were being repeated: the young black girl being taken for a prostitute. She would perform sexual favors on him and he would give her money. Exchange was no robbery.

She could remember laying naked on his king size bed, her legs open wide; he would do a thing to her with his mouth on her vagina. She couldn't understand the pleasure it gave her but she was consoled by the fact that he treated her with gifts. Other times he would take pictures of her naked body, as if he wanted to remember her in her prime. She could tell no one because he was highly respected.

He was a fraud, a pedophile, an abusive Santa Claus. She reminisced and spat out her disgust. She hated that man with every vein inside her. Hated what he had done to her and countless other young girls. He did not penetrate her, but his touch had lingered on her for many years. There was a prison in her mind where he stood, and the only way she could set him free was if he died and she could know for sure he went to hell.

THE EXASPERATED EX

She had waited ten years. Although he had moved on, she still waited. No matter how many men she entertained, there was something special about him, there was something distinct about what they shared.

She was lurking in the dark, hoping that his new woman would break his heart and it'd be her who would pick up the pieces. She despised seeing them together. She saw him post about his new woman all over social media, boasting , calling her his baby. But still, she didn't care. Deep in her heart, she knew he was hers. She rolled her eyes but still managed to click the Like button, her heart filled with hatred and resentment. The distaste in her mouth was growing even stronger, the bitterness was evident but she brushed it aside.

To win him back being a villain even once in her life was a small price to pay. She smiled at the thought and decided she would end them. She just needed one sole window of opportunity to push her way back into his life. She phoned him crying. He was always a good listener and he would be a great confidant for a friend in distress.

ONCE BITTEN, TWICE SHY

She knew what it felt like to be cheated on. She knew what it felt like to be betrayed and pushed to her breaking point. Love had been bittersweet every time she came in contact with it. Trust was often broken and history would repeat itself. She could not let go of all the pain and that was a fact.

Sometimes the memories would start flooding in and she'd feel insecure. She would recheck her figure in the mirror, she would look at photos of herself and ask, "Am I truly beautiful?" She would compare herself to every woman he cheated with, trying to find what they had that she didn't. She would always analyze herself to see if her attitude had been in check. She could not spot a single flaw.

In her eyes, she was perfection, but in his eyes, she obviously had not exceeded his expectations. She would always question her worth and that was natural. Why did people expect her to conceal the pain as if nothing affected her? She would always remember the betrayal and feel sad, she was only human. Her heart had been broken and, repaired it may be, it could never be whole again.

LIFE IS GOOD

She felt like most of her stories were too sad. There were a few out of the compilation that had a happy ending. Life was no fairy tale, but happiness could indeed be a part of her life, so she decided to change the game. She began to change her life, her choices, and embrace a positive aura.

She stepped into the morning breeze, head held high; her strides confident and sure. Inhaling and exhaling the freshness of the day, she felt at ease. Her earphones were plugged in and she was listening to some good Bob Marley.

Life was good. It was good because she claimed it. It was good because she was going to let it be. It was good because, despite her many problems, she also had many blessings. So she smiled to herself and whispered, "Life is good baby girl. Life is good."

STUMBLING IS
STILL PROGRESS

She still had some growing up to do, mentally. Her body was grown, but her mind wasn't. It wasn't a lack of strong encouragement or any deformities. She was just slow. Always moving at a slow pace, always moving slower than others. But it was okay, because not everyone was meant to move fast.

She moved slowly, but nevertheless she kept on moving. She was always aiming for self-improvement, which was key. She knew there was more to life than her current situation. She was delayed but she could never be denied because she had good faith and she always kept her spirit up. For some people, a slower pace toward success seemed negative, but she was never negative. She knew that slow and steady won the race.

She strongly believed that sometimes God had to put a stall on the journey to clear the track of anything that was not of Him. So she waited. She was joyful and always smiling because the longer the stall, the greater the blessings would be.

THE INEVITABLE

She waited for death to come. She knew it would creep up on her when she least expected it. The inevitable, though inescapable, was the hardest pill to swallow. She waited, while her breathing became slower and her strength slowly faded away. She waited patiently. Would she truly rest in peace? That would be a question for another dimension.

She laid flat on her back, legs outstretched and arms knitted to her sides. She was getting in position, she could not escape her fate but unlike many others before her, she had the chance to get her heart, mind, and soul right with God.

She was grateful, though unsure if she was ready to leave her children behind, she was sure they would hold on to the memories and keep them tucked within their hearts forever. It was almost that time, her spirit levitated, her body in pain no more.

CARRY YOUR CROSS

Her lover died suddenly. It was rumored that he had died of a deadly disease. She was left without a shoulder to cry on and an immediate blood test to try to clear her name. She waited for what seemed like an eternity for her results. She did not know what to expect and she couldn't confide in anyone. She was scared and she was confused. They had always shared their bodies intimately without protection; he always said it felt better being bare. She was so hurt, she was extremely angry. She wanted to scream, she wanted to retaliate; she wanted to kill someone. She was at her wit's end, having to take such a loss in life, then to be placed in such a discriminatory position. It was all so overwhelming. She was ready to take someone down, no matter what the cost.

It was her dear mother who consoled her. She embraced her and said, "This is your cross, my child. Carry it! Wear your scars proudly!" She received her results soon after and she prayed before opening the envelope. As she tore the paper apart, tears stained her face. But within her hands she unknowingly held something that would bring her so much joy and peace for she was healthy. She was as clean as a whistle. She was elated, she looked up toward the sky with both hands held high and uttered a gleeful and meaningful, "Thank You!"

BROKEN BOND

She tried to forget the sordid things the woman said to her. She tried to brush aside all the obvious insults. She pushed it all to the back of her mind until she could not take it anymore. She sometimes had regrets of expressing how she felt because the woman made her seem like the devil. The woman played the victim, made her seem cold. The woman cried, she told lies, and she played a manipulative game that tied others around her little finger.

The woman caused people to look at her with great disgust. She had thought the woman to be different, she had viewed her to be kind and impartial. She was glad however to see the type of person she really was. She knew for a fact that she had to keep her at arm's length and watch her back.

She would never be good enough in the woman's eyes. The deed was done, she had crossed a line and there was no turning back. The relationship was ruined, the "bond" was broken forever, regardless of the fact that the woman was indeed her lover's mother.

DON'T LET YOUR CROWN FALL

He called her a stupid prostitute. He told her the most negative things that left her questioning her worth. He insulted her well being. She was so angry at his words that she retaliated and told him he disgusted her. She argued with the father of her child who was being bitter toward her because they no longer shared an intimate relationship.

He had often wanted to visit her house at late hours or take her out for a drink, but she would tell him no. She would not let him hurt her anymore. Not physically, not emotionally. She swore at him over the phone, threatened to call the cops; she said he was a deadbeat and that their daughter was doing just fine without him. She was so caught up in her hysterics that she forgot her daughter was in the room. She hung up and sat down. Head held toward the cold, tiled floor.

She was more upset at herself now because she crossed a line that she promised herself she would never cross. Her daughter came over to her and held her face up. She said, "Mommy, never look down. Your crown will fall. You remember, Mommy? You remember? That's what you told me." She hugged her baby and started sobbing quietly.

She apologized for her behavior and gave her baby a sweet little peck on both cheeks. She had to be mindful of her actions, because her little girl was watching. And she had to be careful, because he was obviously delusional, as she saw his number pop up on her phone screen for the thousandth time.

NO MONEY, NO HONEY

She was a gold digger. Point blank, period. She was unashamed. No matter how many times she was called a prostitute, she did not care. Her motto was "no money, no honey." For her, it was all about the bling, the dazzle, the spotlight. She was not one to ponder on whether or not the man respected her. It was okay if he didn't...as long as he was putting some dollar bills in her purse.

If he was rich, her services would be even greater. A person looking in from the outside would not understand. They would just judge. But if they only knew the little girl she had been before. The little girl neglected by a man who was not yet ready to be a father. The little girl who had to support herself from the age of eight, but who now sat with a master's degree in business on her lap. So was it so bad that, in exchange for a good education, she gave physical pleasure to rich, older men? The question was rhetorical, because she sure as hell did not think so.

BE WHO YOU ARE

She was different. She did not follow the norms set by society or her family. She liked piercings, she liked makeup, she lived to dress provocatively. But behind her appearances stood a humble girl who was not swayed by the world. She was just unique in her own way. No matter how much they judged her, she would not dim her light to make them feel better.

She kept on shining and living the way she wanted. She was walking her own path, on her own journey. She ensured that she was living and not merely existing. she had one shot at life and wanted to make it count, so she would do things the way she wanted. They labeled her a bad girl, but she didn't care. She would embrace who she was with no apologies.

Her life was filled with amazing experiences, memories, and lessons. She was who she was and she would be who she was supposed to be. A bold, eccentric, strong willed, ambitious young woman.

COUNT BLESSINGS, NOT PROBLEMS

She was struggling. Sometimes she did not know where the first meal of the day was coming from. Sometimes she did not know how the bills were going to be paid. Some nights she would cry herself to sleep, because the burdens placed upon her were too heavy. She was trying, though, amid the struggle, she continued to push forward, to create new opportunities for herself. She tried her very best.

She had big dreams. At times she felt as though her dreams were far out of her reach, she did not even know the first step to take toward them. Nevertheless, every morning God woke her up in good health, with great strength and He supplied her every need. Wherever she fell short, her Creator intervened and she was beyond grateful. She knew for sure that her life was not yet over, because each new day brought continuous blessings.

FORGIVENESS HEALS

She looked at the child with pure disgust. The child kept reminding her of her husband's infidelity. How could she see the child and not feel heartbroken? How could she love someone who tore her marriage apart? The worst part, her husband expected her to play a mother's role in the bastard's life. "He must be crazy !" she said angrily to herself.

She hated the child and so the child grew to hate her. She confided in her eldest sister about this and her sister replied, "Anything you put inside, is what you will get out, negative or positive. Be careful, that is all I'm saying." She never understood what her sister meant, instead she got upset and as the days flew by she became old, grumpy, and bitter. The grudge she held had consumed her, making her heart, and eventually her outer appearance ugly. She was no longer the beautiful, jovial woman she had once been. She was a woman of faith unable to forgive. She chose hate instead of love, and in the end she lost the spark to her soul.

AN EXPERIENCED WOMAN

She lost a part of herself a few years ago and it was dreadful. She'd taken two pills that ended the life growing inside her. Her choice? No. But still, she'd done it. Regrets? She was not sure, because whether she wanted to admit it or not, she had been in no position to take on such responsibility; she had only been a teenager. When the blood flowed between her legs, she had prayed and asked God for forgiveness. She knew He had forgiven her because a few years later He blessed her womb again.

She felt as though she was well equipped for the journey after all the pain she'd endured. She knew her mistakes had redesigned her and her views. She had learned about compassion, acceptance and respecting other's opinions. She would not judge, because she had been there. She could relate to nearly any problem a woman encountered in her daily life. She understood the beauty beneath her flaws. Her lessons gave her in depth wisdom that would last a lifetime.

She was no loser. She was an experienced woman. She had been and done everything that was "wrong." She had been in the gutter. Her scars were a testimony. Her story was a life changer to the ears that were meant to listen and understand.

LADY OF THE NIGHT

She felt the music go straight to her soul. The lights were on her. All eyes were glued to her, she was under the influence, transfixed in her own haze. Her body twisted around the long, silver pole. The small stage was her altar, she owned the night; she felt powerful. She gyrated her hips, swayed from side to side, her motions defined, her stance on point. Her attention was drawn to a man standing in a corner she could feel him watching her, he never once took his eyes off her. The room was dark but their eyes made contact. She held his gaze for a while and she thought she recognized him though he wasn't close enough to be sure.

Ten minutes later she exited the stage while the next performer was summoned by the hostess. As she made her way through the crowd toward the dressing room, a cold, sweaty hand grabbed on to her. She turned around to see a very familiar face. Shock ran through her like a thousand electrical volts. It was him, the man she had married. The man she never deserved. He had found her yet again in a most unfortunate state. She knew it made no sense for her to go home with him and get cleaned up. She would watch as he picked up the pieces over and over again. He would try to rebuild something that was meant to stay broken. She never wanted to be a loyal wife or a devoted mother. She wanted to be a lady of the night, no expectations, no strings attached.

TILL DEATH DO US PART

She was dressed in her best white dress. Hair and makeup done to perfection. She would look her best for him, that wouldn't change even though he was no longer with her. She sat in the front row of the chapel surrounded by their families and closest friends. She had flashbacks of another special day similar to the setting before her. Their friends and family, the decorations, but not the sadness that lingered. Soft whimpers could be heard, handkerchiefs were stained with tears, tongues bled from words left unsaid. Hearts were broken, grief was evident. Her head down toward her lap. She made circles with her fingers on the satin material of her clothing. She did not know how to come to terms with the reality, until she was interrupted by a woman crying hysterically. The woman was dressed in a maternity gown, she had both arms wrapped comfortably around her tummy. The woman was with child. She needed no introduction to know who she was, because she had done her research. The woman was the reason for her husband's demise. One swift hit-man, two bullets straight to the head. She meant what she had told him on happier days: "Till death do we part, my love; till death do we part."

BE FREE AND TRULY HEAL

He let her leave. He watched her while she packed her suitcase; he followed her outside but he never stopped her. He sat on the steps while she strode away with tears in her eyes. He could have begged her to stay, but didn't. Even though he was sad, he was a bit relieved. He wanted his freedom to live a selfish, self-absorbed life. He had tried to show her that she deserved better than him with his constant cheating, but still she stayed.

For several years. On and off with their relationship. She finally found the courage to walk away and he could not rob her of that. He had to accept the reality and be happy for her growth. He had to set her free from all the pain of the toxic love he had given her. This was why he let her go, so she could truly heal. She'd only pretend to be happy with him, she could forgive him for all the hurt and pain, but she would never forget. He whispered to himself, "Sometimes holding on does more damage than letting go."

ELEVATION REQUIRES SEPARATION

She knew some friends would come and go. She knew some people only pretended to like her so they could have a front row seat to her life and decisions. She knew some people in her circle were not really for her but for others by giving others the support she craved, being there for others but never for her. She watched her "friends" roll with the same people who spoke badly about them behind their backs and she could do nothing but shake her head in shame.

She had been loyal to people who never deserved her loyalty, so she decided to mind her own business and keep it moving. She had to learn the hard way that some people could never be happy for her, no matter how she tried to show them the truest parts of her. Amid her struggles, she could count the few who really stood by her through and through. Most, though, rejoiced silently at her downfall and were dumb enough to think that she didn't know.

She continued to push forward. She was smarter than the fraudulent pretenders, the plastics, the evil-minded and jealous hearted. She gave thanks that they showed their true colors in the moment of her shine because it made loving them from a distance so much easier.

SELF-CARE IS NOT SELFISH

She had to focus on her, as selfish as it sounded, she had to put her needs before everyone else's. She kept trying to find happiness in other people, not grasping that it had to come from within her. Everyone wasn't meant to understand her solitude and even though some felt hurt by her focus, she could not stray from her vision to make anyone comfortable.

She knew that misery loved company, so she made no time for those who tried to hurt others with their tyrannical ways. She learned to ignore the hate and the fake. She learned to love her own company. She was being selfish, but that was okay, because she had work to do. She remembered who she was, and so she changed the game.

HOLDING IT TOGETHER

He lied, and it wasn't that simple. He had truly disappointed her, he had her questioning how much she meant to him. Did she not deserve the truth? He had done some damage deeper than what the surface would portray. Years of constant mistakes and flaws. He had always been perfect to her through everything she thought she ever wanted, everything she thought she ever needed. She had been the one to put them back together, she forgave him and saved them over and over again.

Sometimes, it felt one sided to her and that was what hurt the most. She gave the most. She was always giving. There was no denying that she was in love and he couldn't even make eye contact with her. Deep down, she knew it was over in so many ways. Her heart was like a cracked glass. It could not be mended, and overtime it would just continue to shatter to pieces. She was broken, but somehow she still managed to hold herself together. The same thing that broke her, made her stronger.

A GIRL JUST WANTS HAPPINESS

She was not being unreasonable. She was just tired of waiting. He always kept her waiting. He never saw the damage that his actions caused, but she was bruised by them more than he could ever know. It was easy for him to give so much of himself to others, but it always felt as though he withheld some of himself from her, and it drove her crazy.

She wanted to be happy, that was a fact, but it never sat well with her when she realized that his happy place was seldom with her. He was never on time, he was always too late; he was always preoccupied. She was tired of the excuses and the lack of effort. Sometimes she didn't understand why she held on, why she worried, why she even bothered with him. She was disappointed too many times, when all she wanted was happiness.

HELP A SISTER IN NEED

She knew what hungry days were like. She could remember them now and smile. She reminisced on the evenings when all she had was ramen noodles to eat. She would cook them up and consume them as though they were the finest delicacies in the world. She was always grateful because she had something; some people had nothing.

She watched from a distance as everyone passed the homeless woman who was begging for spare change. Some people spat at her, some threw curse words in her direction. She thought to herself, "If only they knew what a single act of kindness can do." She had been the lady on the street, helpless, lost, and confused. She reached into her purse and took out all the money that she could find and strode over to the desperate woman. "Be blessed, my sister, eat and be merry. It gets better." She shared with her some kind words, a warm hug , and a comforting smile.

SONS ARE ANCHORS

She felt crazy. Destructive thoughts ran through her mind. She could not sleep; it was 3 a.m. and she had been up all night. Her eyes were wide open, wet from the tears she had fought so hard to hold back. She couldn't pretend anymore, she was unhappy and there was no denying it. She felt her heart tugging at her chest, she could literally feel the pain eating her alive and there was nothing she could do about it. Her cup was full, filled with regrets, heartbreaks, and disappointments.

She was at the peak of her breaking point, no turning back. Too many words left unsaid, toxic emotions bottled up inside, and too many meaningless apologies. She sat mumbling to herself, trying to make sense of the pain she felt. She tried to wrap her head around it all, but she still never understood what she had done to deserve such betrayal. She thought about being a savage, but she couldn't. No matter what she wanted to prove to the man who didn't appreciate her, there was a man not yet grown who was watching her every move. Her son. He had changed her, he had kept her stable, he had kept her sane.

A STUPID MISTAKE

She fell for him. Hard. She had never expected to, he was taken by someone very close to her, it was wrong. Or was it? Why had he taken a liking to her? What did he expect to gain? She never knew, but she just decided to go with the flow. It never mattered to her that she was betraying another woman. She owed her no loyalty; it was her man who did. She hissed her teeth at the thought. He was handsome and very charming, kind and compassionate. Everything she needed in a man, he was it. She would daydream all the time about his looks and kisses, so she entertained him at the expense of another woman's pain. She broke the ultimate girl code, but his woman deserved it because she was too spoiled and always got what she wanted. Little did she know, he only viewed her as temporary.

She was a mistake that happened because of too much close contact. She flaunted too much of her seductive body before him and he was a weak man who could not deny the lust he felt. Pure infatuation, was all it was to him. His woman was still in the loop because his heart belonged to her. She kept popping up. It was messy, and she had no choice but to give him an ultimatum. He had to choose who it was he wanted to be with, and if she had known what his decision would be, she would never have slept with her best friend's boyfriend.

CANDLELIGHT

She had a single candle burning in the room. The only light that was present in the darkness. She sat on the floor in silence, giving the voices in her head a chance to speak. Her thoughts were running wild, destructively wild. She felt misplaced and unsure of her purpose. The candlelight, although dimmed, kept her sane. It meant more to her than just a regular lit candle. It was her remedy.

Though the darkness consumed her, one speck of light before her meant there was still hope. Hope amid the turmoil, the doubts, and the unforgettable mistakes. She was surrounded by sharp razors, bottles of alcohol, pills that meant overdose or sudden death. She prayed that the candle would keep burning, because if it ever stopped, she would be no more.

She watched as it kept burning , and burning , and burning. No matter how much it shrunk, it still kept burning. The candle was depicting her current situation. No matter how belittled she felt, she had to keep the fire within her burning. She had to keep shining luminously.

UNHAPPY HOME

She was unhappy. She was done pretending. She had to move on, she just had to. It was their one year anniversary. She sat at the polished dining table, waiting for him to get home. He was late and she knew he'd be intoxicated but she still had to try having a conversation with him, drunk or not. She had to let the frustration out. She had to feel as though she could breathe again.

She was suffocating. Living a lie was hard. She had to pretend to be the happy wife, the devoted woman who was being loved and cared for in the right way. Little did her family know of what happened behind the closed doors of their marital home. Heated arguments, constant fighting, and physical abuse. She was exhausted.

His car pulled up in the driveway. As she heard the key in the front door, she practiced all she would say in her mind. She was going to let it all out, pack her things, and leave. She closed her eyes and prepared for the worst as the man she once adored entered the ruins of what was once a happy home.

SCARRED

She was scarred at only a few months old, by parents who were not cautious, who did not know what unnecessary fights could cause. She tried not to hate them, but every time she saw her image in the mirror she was saddened and she became angry. Her forehead was deformed. Doctors had tried to fix it, but the damage was irreversible. As she grew up, the scar grew with her, never leaving and always visible.

She tried to hide it by combing her hair with bangs, but still it was always there when she got home and wrapped her hair up to go to sleep. She wished it would go away, she sometimes cried silently. It was weakening her self esteem because she never felt beautiful. But she was not only beautiful, she was special. It took her a very long time to accept her scar and when she finally did, she wore it proudly. The scar was a reminder of all she had been through, of a time in her life when she had survived. She was without doubt, a true survivor.

AFTERWORD

I want to extend a big thank you to everyone who took the time to read my pieces. It was a real privilege to write this book, and I'm happy to be able to share my work with the world. Passion is undeniable: even when I didn't know why I was writing, I just kept writing.

Inspiration first comes from within you, life just gives you a push in the direction you are meant to go, but it is our duty to move forward and affect our destiny. Never give up, just work on your craft no matter what it may be.

I am truly humbled to have been given the opportunity to write such an amazing book that most women can relate to. The title SHE is an acronym meaning strength, humility, and endurance. Some of my characters find the strength within to overcome many obstacles. All of my characters are modest in all that they do, and all that they've endured.

This is the start of a new journey, a new chapter, a new life. Brace your-selves, a new writer is on the rise. I intend to continue working on my craft, and I only hope to get better with time.

ABOUT THE AUTHOR

Patrice Simpson, a Jamaican native, cultivated her passion for writing amidst the scenic beauty of the "land of wood and water." Her early affinity for reading set the stage, but it was during her pregnancy that she discovered solace, igniting a profound love for the art of writing. Navigating life's challenges, Patrice skillfully transformed her experiences into captivating narratives.

Her writing journey expanded beyond personal reflections to include the stories of the women in her family and community, culminating in the creation of her impactful book, "SHE."

Remarkably, Patrice is now a two-time self-published author. She currently operates a successful writing service, showcasing her expertise and dedication to the craft. With a heartfelt aspiration, Patrice Simpson hopes that her words become a source of inspiration for others on their own journeys.

9 789768 277862